W9-DJG-171

Wild Flowers of Connecticut

Wild Flowers of Connecticut

BY DR. JOHN E. KLIMAS, JR.

PUBLISHED FOR AUDUBON SOCIETY,
STATE OF CONNECTICUT

WALKER AND COMPANY

NEW YORK

To Roy and Margot Larsen of Fairfield, who, because of their love of nature and desire to preserve a part of the historic Connecticut landscape, donated the land that forms the Larsen Audubon Sanctuary, in which the flowers described in this book were studied and photographed.

First published in the United States of America in 1968 by Walker and Company, a division of the Walker Publishing Company, Inc.
Published simultaneously in Canada by The Ryerson Press, Toronto.

Printed in the United States of America

Table of Contents

Introduction

IN the northeastern part of the United States, wild flowers form a colorful part of our natural environment for at least six months of the year. Because of their color, variety, and beauty, they generate a sense of curiosity that leads the amateur naturalist or casual hiker to want to learn more about them. The purpose of this book is to enable one who has had no previous botanical training to identify the most common and widely distributed wild flowers found specifically in Connecticut but also generally in most of New England, New York, and New Jersey. It contains a selection of photographs and commentary on those herbaceous wild flowers that, because of color, size, or number, the amateur is most likely to see.

Learning to recognize wild flowers is only half the fun of this type of activity. Most flowers also have a story to tell about the origins of their common or scientific names or their uses in folk medicine. This affords one the opportunity to learn about herbal medicine and folklore, which are such an interesting aspect of the history of this part of the country. Many of the common names of plants are derived from the "doctrine of signatures," an antiquated theory which stated that the outward appearance of an object indicated its special properties that could be used in magic or in healing. Thus, for example, medicines and potions prepared from plants having heart-shaped leaves were utilized in an attempt to cure heart diseases.

All flowers have been listed using the common name and scientific name (genus and species), along with their family affiliation. This nomenclature conforms with that found in the eighth edition of *Gray's Manual of Botany*.

To avoid baffling or discouraging the beginner, this elementary guidebook minimizes the technical jargon of the botanist and uses color as the key to identification. Although color has its limitations, it serves the beginner well. Other botanical features that may help in identification—such as size of flower; height of plant; habitat; and characteristics of fruit, foliage, and stem—are also described.

Not only are the flowers arranged by color, but also the flowers of the same color are arranged by the seasons in which they usually first appear. In the spring we look for the first flowers in the woods. They are given a head start by the warmth of the natural mulch of fallen leaves; and, since most are bulbs or tubers, there is no waiting for the germination of seeds. Toward the end of May and the beginning of June we see a lesser number of flowers in the woods, because the trees have developed their foliage and the shade prevents the growth of all but the shade-tolerant plants. The place to look for wild flowers at this time is out in the open woods or in the meadows. Many of these plants continue to bloom until the fall, whereas others are short-lived.

When you have found a flower you would like to identify, observe the predominant coloration. Check through that section of the book containing the photographs of flowers of that coloration. Sometimes it is difficult to determine the color of a flower, especially since blues, purples, and pinks gradually blend one into the other. In this case make a decision for one color, and if the flower is not identified, try another color section that might include it. Because of the large number of species in some genera, the particular species you have found might not be illustrated, but at least you will know what kind of a flower it is. Also remember that you might find a fairly rare or inconspicuous plant that is not described in this guide. The following works can be used in these identifications and for more technical information: Harold W. Rickett, *Wild Flowers of the United States: The Northeastern States*, 2 vols. (New York, McGraw-Hill Book Company, 1966); and Edgar T. Wherry, *Wild Flower Guide: Northeastern and Midland United States* (New York, Doubleday & Company, 1948).

Wild flowers add that color and zest to a landscape that would otherwise be rather dull. In an effort to bring some of this natural charm into the home or cultivated garden, people sometimes pick the flowers or attempt to transplant the entire plant. In most cases transplanting is an exercise in futility, since the casual-appearing requirements for the growth of wild flowers are actually fairly stringent. Overpicking can lead to the eventual extinction of a species, since the annuals depend upon their flowers to produce seed for next year's crop of flowers. Even the perennial, which grows from a rootstock or tuber, can suffer from overpicking, because invariably their leaves are plucked along with the flower, and the underground parts of these plants depend upon the leaves to furnish nutrients for producing future flowers. To ensure that wild flowers will always be a part of man's natural environment, "Take nothing but pictures, leave nothing but your footsteps."

JOHN E. KLIMAS, JR.

Fairfield, Connecticut

1. *White Flowers*

W-1 TRAILING ARBUTUS *(Epigaea repens)* Heath family
Height: Prostrate. Flower: ½″ diameter.
Season: Early spring (p.21)

This prostrate perennial with thick, oval-shaped, evergreen leaves is usually found in shaded woods on rocky, well-drained banks. Because of the shape and color of the leaves, this plant is often called "ground laurel." The delicate white blossoms, which appear in early spring, are produced at the ends of the branches and are extremely fragrant. Unfortunately, the trailing arbutus is becoming rare in this part of the country. This is rather ironic, since another name for the plant is "mayflower," because it was believed to have been the first flower the Pilgrims saw after their initial harsh winter in New England.

W-2 WOOD ANEMONE *(Anemone quinquefolia)* Buttercup family
Height: 8″–10″. Flower: 1″ diameter.
Season: Early spring (p.21)

The wood anemone is a small plant found in open woods in moderately rich soil. The more basal leaves are divided into five-pointed leaflets. The four to seven white "petals" are petal-like sepals. Because of their slender stems, the solitary flower trembles in the slightest breeze; hence the common name, "windflower." In ancient times it was believed that the wind that passed over a field of anemones was poisoned and would cause sickness in anyone inhaling this air. This is perhaps the reason that the Persians adopted this flower as their emblem of illness.

W-3 RUE ANEMONE *(Anemonella thalictroides)* Buttercup family
Height: 4″–8″. Flower: ¾″ diameter.
Season: Early spring (p.21)

This plant is often confused with the wood anemone because they are found in the same habitat. The white flower is also composed of five to ten sepals. However, the rue anemone produces a cluster of flowers instead of a solitary blossom, and the leaves are divided into three round-lobed leaflets.

W-4   DWARF GINSENG *(Panax trifolius)*   Ginseng family
Height: 3″–6″. Flower: ⅛″ diameter; 15–25 in spherical cluster.
Season: Early spring   (p.21)

This low-growing herb is found along streams or in damp depressions in the
woods. The leaves are composed of three or five leaflets. The underground stem,
or tuber, is edible and pungent-tasting. For this reason the plant is often called
groundnut.

W-5   BLOODROOT *(Sanguinaria canadensis)*   Poppy family
Height: 6″–10″. Flower: 1″–1½″ diameter.
Season: Early spring   (p.21)

This short-lived flower is unusual because of the waxy, white color of its eight to
twelve petals. The single leaf, heart-shaped with five to nine prominent lobes, is
wrapped around the flower bud as it emerges from the ground; it expands only
after the flower has bloomed. The plant is often found growing in clusters on
shaded banks in rich woods. The rootstock and stem contain a bright-red,
poisonous sap, to which the common name refers. It is said that the Indians used
the sap not only as a dye for their garments and handiwork but also as a war paint
when necessary.

W-6   DUTCHMAN'S BREECHES *(Dicentra cucullaria)* Fumitory family
Height: 6″–10″. Flower: ¾″ long.
Season: Early spring   (p.21)

This plant is best found growing in clusters on rocky ledges. The common name
is derived from the four to twelve two-spurred flowers on an arched stem that
look like white pantaloons on a clothesline, hung with the yellow-belted waist
down and the ankles up. The basal leaves are finely divided and fernlike.

W-7   WHITE TRILLIUM *(Trillium grandiflorum)*   Lily family
Height: 8″–14″. Flower: 3″–4″ diameter.
Season: Early spring   (p.22)

Trilliums are characterized by having three leaves, three sepals, and three petals.
The white trillium is one of the most striking of early spring flowers because of
its large size. Although the flower is white when it first appears, the petals gradually change in color, so that after a time they become pink or dull rose. Look for
these flowers on wooded slopes in rich woods.

W-8   SAXIFRAGE *(Saxifraga virginiensis)*   Saxifrage family
Height: 8″–15″. Flower: ¼″ long; branching cluster.
Season: Early spring   (p.22)

The crevices of rocky cliffs and hillsides are the preferred habitat of this plant. The hairy, leafless stem bearing the flowers near the top springs from a basal rosette of paddle-shaped leaves. Saxifrage is a combination of two Latin words meaning "stone breaker," an obvious reference to its supposed ability to disintegrate the rock upon which it is growing. Observing this, herb doctors believed that the root of this plant could be used as a medicine to disintegrate kidney stones.

W-9   SPRING BEAUTY *(Claytonia virginica)*   Portulaca family
Height: 4″–8″. Flower: ¾″ diameter.
Season: Early spring   (p.22)

These delicate harbingers of spring grow in such large masses in open woods or meadows that they look like patches of unmelted snow. However, the five-petaled flowers with pink veins open only in bright sunlight, so they are not seen on cloudy days. The two grasslike leaves rise from a starchy bulb that was eaten by the Indians.

W-10   WILD LILY-OF-THE-VALLEY *(Maianthemum canadense)*
Height: 4″–6″. Flower: ¼″ diameter; 15–25 in a cluster.   Lily family
Season: Spring   (p.22)

This plant is first seen as widespread patches of pointed, oval leaves on zigzag stems covering the floor of cool, moist woods. The stalk of white flowers appears in May; during the summer small clusters of speckled pale-red berries are produced. This plant is also called "Canada mayflower," since it grows in mass profusion in the Canadian woodlands.

W-11   SOLOMON'S SEAL *(Polygonatum pubescens)*   Lily family
Height: 1′–2′. Flower: ½″ long.
Season: Spring   (p.22)

These plants are common wherever there is a moist slope in open woods. The common name comes from the shape of the scar left by each previous year's stalk on the underground stem, which resembles the seal impressed in wax on official documents in former times. The arched stem has alternating lance-shaped leaves. The small, green-white, bell-shaped flowers originate from the base of each leaf and hang down singly or in pairs along the stem. During the summer dark-blue berries develop.

W-12   FALSE SOLOMON'S SEAL *(Smilacina racemosa)*   Lily family
Height: 2'–3'. Flower: ¼" diameter; terminal cluster.
Season: Spring   (p.22)

This plant resembles the true Solomon's Seal in general shape and habitat. It differs in that the arched stem is zigzag in shape and the white flowers are found in a showy cluster at the end of the stem. In the fall the flower cluster becomes a mass of red berries, which are quite conspicuous even in the colorful woods.

W-13   WILD STRAWBERRY *(Fragaria virginiana)*   Rose family
Height: Prostrate. Flower: ½" diameter.
Season: Spring   (p.23)

Wild strawberry resembles the cultivated strawberry in being a creeping vine with leaves of three dark-green leaflets with coarse margins and white, five-petaled flowers. However, the fruit is much smaller than that obtained from the cultivated plant but is far superior in taste. This plant is found in rather dry soil in fields and on hillsides.

W-14   WHITE BANEBERRY *(Actaea pachypoda)*   Buttercup family
Height: 1'–2'. Flower: ¼" diameter; terminal cluster.
Season: Spring   (p.23)

In the open woods we seldom notice the baneberry, not because it is that rare a plant but because its flower cluster is rather inconspicuous above the main mass of sharp-toothed leaflets of the compound leaves. However, when the fruit ripens in the late summer, this is an eyecatching cluster of white, oval, berrylike fruit with a black tip; hence the common name "doll's eyes." These berries are poisonous, which accounts for the name "baneberry."

W-15   MAYSTAR *(Trientalis borealis)*   Primrose family
Height: 5"–7". Flower: ½" diameter.
Season: Spring   (p.23)

Cool, hilly woods are the optimum habitat for this plant. The white starflower, as it is often called, is star-shaped, with five to nine pointed petals found above a whorl of six to eight taper-pointed leaves.

W-16   WILD SARSAPARILLA *(Aralia nudicaulis)*   Ginseng family
Height: 12"–15". Flower: ¼" diameter; spherical cluster.
Season: Spring   (p.23)

The roots of this plant are aromatic and were often used as a substitute for true sarsaparilla flavoring. The round clusters of greenish-white flowers are rather inconspicuous beneath the single leaf, which is divided into three compound leaflets. Look for this plant in rich, open woods.

W-17 DAISY *(Chrysanthemum leucanthemum)* Composite family
Height: 2′–3′. Flower: 1½″ diameter.
Season: Spring (p.23)

This is a native of Europe that escaped cultivation when brought to this country. It is a member of the large composite family, characterized by each single flower actually being a grouping of many small flowers of two kinds—ray flowers and disk flowers. The mass of small disk flowers makes up the yellow center, which is surrounded by the petal-like white ray flowers. It is indeed a joyful sight to see a field of daisies, but farmers and dairymen find them a nuisance, since they are difficult to eradicate and ruin good pastureland.

W-18 YARROW *(Achillea millefolium)* Composite family
Height: 1′–2′. Flower: ¼″ diameter; flat-head cluster.
Season: Spring (p.23)

A common roadside plant, the yarrow thrives in dry soil. Although the flower is not very attractive, the alternate leaves are finely dissected and feathery in appearance and the plant is often mistaken for a fern. Yarrow is a European perennial that escaped cultivation when it was brought to this country for its supposed medicinal value: the aromatic leaves were chewed as a remedy for toothache.

W-19 FLEABANE *(Erigeron spp.)* Composite family
Height: 2′–3′. Flower: 1″ diameter.
Season: Spring (p.24)

The fleabanes are a weed of the open field and are usually found along with daisies, which they resemble in miniature. However, the ray flowers may range in color from white to lavender, and the narrow, elliptical leaves are without stalks and are attached directly to the hairy stem. The common name of these plants is derived from the belief that when dried and burned they would be a good insect repellent. Also plants were hung in country cottages for this reason.

W-20 MAYAPPLE *(Podophyllum peltatum)* Barberry family
Height: 1′–1½′. Flower: 1″–1½″ diameter; nodding.
Season: Spring (p.24)

The plant, which grows in dense patches in open woods, produces two fan-shaped leaves which hang in a horizontal position; hence its other common name, "umbrella leaf." A single, nodding, white, waxy flower is produced in the fork formed by the two leaf stalks. In the summer the "apple," which is really a juicy yellow berry, ripens. The plant was much sought after during the Middle Ages, when it was called "mandrake" and was said to have magic properties.

W-21   SPOTTED WINTERGREEN *(Chimaphila maculata)*
        Height: 4″–6″. Flower: ¾″ diameter; nodding.   Wintergreen family
        Season: Early summer   (p.24)

While most flowers are blooming in the sunny fields and meadows, a walk in the dark dry woods in July will be rewarded with the sight of clusters of small white flowers nodding above leathery, dark-green, white-striped leaves. Another common name for this plant is of Indian origin—"pipsissewa."

W-22   PARTRIDGE BERRY *(Mitchella repens)*   Madder family
        Height: Prostrate. Flower: ¼″ diameter; pairs.
        Season: Early summer   (p.24)

This small, creeping evergreen with small, dark-green, oval leaves is found in the densely shaded parts of the woods, where it may form a thick mat. The white flowers occur in pairs, joined at their bases so that the single red berry formed later in the summer is actually two fused fruits. Because it can tolerate shade, is easily transplanted, and is evergreen, it is a much-used plant in indoor terrariums.

W-23   QUEEN ANNE'S LACE *(Daucus carota)*   Carrot family
        Height: 1′–3′. Flower: ⅛″ diameter; flat-head cluster.
        Season: Early summer   (p.24)

Another European immigrant, this plant closely resembles yarrow in appearance and habitat. The common name originated when someone in England decided the blossoms resembled Queen Anne's lace headdress. The leaves are feathery, and if you look closely at the center of the flower cluster, you will notice that one of the small flowers is dark purple. This plant had economic value, since it is the wild plant from which early man developed the common garden carrot. Crush a leaf between your fingers and note the odor of carrot.

W-24   HORSE NETTLE *(Solanum carolinense)*   Nightshade family
        Height: Sprawling vine. Flower: ¾″ diameter.
        Season: Early summer   (p.24)

This plant is found in sandy soil in meadows and fields. Although the plant is not a member of the rose family, the stems, branches, and even the underside of the deeply lobed, lance-shaped leaves are covered with prickles. The star-shaped flower produces bright-yellow berries in the fall.

W-25 TALL MEADOW RUE *(Thalictrum polygamum)* Buttercup family
Height: 3′–11′. Flower: ¼″ long; terminal cluster.
Season: Summer (p.25)

The tall, white, feathery clusters of flowers in wet meadows call our attention to this plant. A close look at the flowers, however, reveals that there are no petals and that the attractive tassels are composed of numerous white stamens. The feathery appearance of the plant is enhanced by the finely divided compound leaves, which are bluntly lobed.

W-26 MEADOWSWEET *(Spiraea latifolia)* Rose family
Height: 2′–5′. Flower: ¼″ diameter; dense terminal cluster.
Season: Summer (p.25)

The normal habitat for this woody shrub is the moist meadow or wooded field. The distinguishing feature of this meadow plant is smooth, reddish stems, and branches with dark-green, oval, sparsely toothed leaves topped by the dense cluster of small white flowers.

W-27 PEARLY EVERLASTING *(Anaphalis margaritacea)*
Composite family
Height: 1′–2′. Flower: ½″ diameter; terminal cluster.
Season: Summer (p.25)

Another plant found in dry, open fields is the white, woolly pearly everlasting. What appears to be a flower with a yellow center and white petals is actually a cluster of minute yellow flowers surrounded by numerous pearly-white scales (bracts). The common name, "everlasting," comes from the observation that although the stem and thin, lance-shaped leaves are green, they are covered with so much woolly material that they look like dead, preserved plants. If you crush a leaf between your fingers, it will emit a slight lemon scent.

W-28 INDIAN PIPES *(Monotropa uniflora)* Heath family
Height: 4″–8″. Flower: ½″ diameter; nodding.
Season: Summer (p.25)

The more rain that falls during the summer, the more often we can find this plant in the rich woods. Because it lacks chlorophyll, all parts of the plant—stems, leaves, and single, nodding flower—are white. Being a saprophyte, it derives its nourishment from the dead organic matter in which it is growing. Because of its unusual waxy-white appearance, it is often picked. However, it soon turns black when picked, which accounts for its Indian name, "corpse plant."

W-29   POKEWEED *(Phytolacca americana)*   Poke family
Height: 3′–10′. Flower: ⅜″ diameter.
Season: Summer   (p.25)

The flowers and berries are found at the same time on the same stalk on this plant. Actually, the flower is devoid of petals but has five white sepals. A common plant of fallow fields and waste places, the succulent purple stems and green, lance-shaped leaves are poisonous when eaten by man or cattle. The clusters of dark berries that develop are also poisonous, but they have found some use as a primitive dye and at one time an alcohol solution of the juices was used as a treatment for rheumatism. Twigs of the plant were worn as campaign emblems by the followers of President Polk, even though the names are spelled differently.

W-30   ARROWHEAD *(Sagittaria latifolia)*   Arrowhead family
Height: 1′–2′. Flower: 1″ diameter.
Season: Summer   (p.25)

The peculiar arrow-shaped leaf is the reason for the common and scientific names (*Sagitta* is Latin for "arrow") for this aquatic plant that is found along ponds and the margins of sluggish streams. The conspicuous male flowers grow in whorls of three along a common stalk, with the whorl of three inconspicuous female flowers below. The stout underground stem of this plant not only provides a source of food for many types of waterfowl; because of its high starch content, it was used as a food source by the Algonquin Indians, and the men in the Lewis and Clark expedition used it as a substitute for bread.

W-31   RATTLESNAKE PLANTAIN *(Goodyera pubescens)*   Orchid family
Height: 6″–12″. Flower: ¼″ long; spikelike cluster.
Season: Summer   (p.26)

A fairly rare member of the orchid family, this plant is found blooming in dry woods in the summer. The common name is derived from the basal oval leaves with their network of white lines. They were thought to resemble snakeskin and therefore were supposed to be effective against snakebite if chewed or applied to the bite. In fact, the Indian had such faith in their curative powers that he would allow a poisonous snake to bite him for a sum of money if he had some leaves available for medicinal purposes. Because of the attractive basal leaves and the fact that the plant is easy to transplant, it is often used in terrariums.

W-32 BONESET *(Eupatorium perfoliatum)* Composite family
Height: 2′–5′. Flower: ¼″ diameter; flat-head cluster.
Season: Late summer (p.26)

The unusual feature of this plant is the way the hairy stem seems to grow through the opposite, lance-shaped leaves that are united at their bases so that they surround the stem. Hence the specific name *perfoliatum*, Latin for "through the leaf." This unique characteristic is also responsible for the common name "boneset," since herb doctors believed that plants with united leaves could aid in uniting broken or fractured bones. Look for the flat-headed cluster of white flowers in moist meadows in the late summer, along with the goldenrods and Joe-Pye-weeds.

W-33 WHITE WOODLAND ASTER *(Aster divaricatus)*
Height: 2′–3′. Flower: ¾″ diameter. Composite family
Season: Late summer (p.26)

The asters are a large and difficult group to identify; only a few of the more common species are described in this book. Although most asters appear in meadows and along the edges of woods in the fall, this white aster blooms in the shaded woods in late summer. It is distinguished by its dark-brown or purple zigzag stem and sharply toothed, lance-shaped, dark-veined leaves.

W-34 HEATH ASTER *(Aster ericoides)* Composite family
Height: 1′–4′. Flower: ½″ diameter.
Season: Late summer (p.26)

This white aster is found on the borders of dry fields. The plant is easily recognized because it has a bushy appearance and the small, stiff, crowded leaves are covered with minute gray hairs. If you see a grayish bush covered with numerous small white flowers in the late summer, you have found the heath aster.

W-35 TURTLEHEAD *(Chelone glabra)* Figwort family
Height: 2′–5′. Flower: 1″–1½″ long; terminal cluster.
Season: Late summer (p.26)

This plant thrives in wet, open woods and along streams. The generic name, *Chelone*, is the Greek word for "tortoise." The white, two-lipped flowers, resembling the head of a turtle, are clustered at the end of a single stalk with opposite, sharp-toothed, lance-shaped leaves. An ointment to relieve itching has been made from these leaves.

2. *Green Flowers*

G-1   JACK-IN-THE-PULPIT *(Arisaema triphyllum)*   Arum family
Height: 1′–2′. Flower: Inconspicuous; within spathe.
Season: Spring   (p.26)

A favorite of children, this spring flower is a member of the same family as the earlier blooming skunk cabbage. The tall green "pulpit" (spathe) is streaked with purple or brown and arches over "Jack" (spadix), contained within it. The small, inconspicuous flowers, which may be male and/or female, are found clustered at "Jack's" feet. When one walks through the damp woodland habitat of this plant, the flower may be hidden by the one or two long-stalked leaves, divided into three leaflets. However, during the late summer, with the leaves dead, the flower is replaced by a glossy red fruit.

G-2   CUCUMBER ROOT *(Medeola virginiana)*   Lily family
Height: 1′–2′. Flower: ⅜″ diameter.
Season: Spring   (p.27)

Because the flowers are small and green, the plant itself is often recognized before the flower. The long slender stem has two whorls of leaves; the upper whorl usually has three narrow leaves and the lower whorl five to nine larger leaves. The small flower, found on long stalks above the upper whorl of leaves, has small green petals curved outward. The natural habitat for the cucumber root is the moist woods. The white, tuberous rootstock has a cucumberlike flavor; hence its common name. Its generic name honors the ancient sorceress Medea, because the plant was believed to have great curative powers.

Other plants whose flowers may appear green at some time during their development: Solomon's seal, wild sarsaparilla, and pokeweed.

3. *Red Flowers*

R-1 RED TRILLIUM *(Trillium erectum)* Trillium family
Height: 6″–9″. Flower: 2″ diameter; nodding.
Season: Spring (p.27)

Since these flowers are in bloom about the time the robins come back in the spring, they are commonly called "wake-robins." Like most members of the trillium family, the plant springs from an underground stem, the stalk of which bears three broad leaves and a flower that has three petals and three sepals. The plant is often overlooked in the open woodlands in which it is found because the flower droops from an arched stalk. Although the flower is handsome, its rank odor has gained it the other common names of "wet-dog trillium" and "stinking Benjamin"!

R-2 WILD COLUMBINE *(Aquilegia canadensis)* Buttercup family
Height: 1′–2′. Flower: 1½″ long.
Season: Spring (p.27)

The delicate grace and poise of this flower is heightened by the ruggedness of its natural habitat, which is the rocky slopes of open woods. The nodding flowers are at the ends of rather tall stems with delicately compound leaves. The derivation of the generic name *(aquila,* Latin for "eagle") and the common name *(columba,* Latin for "dove") is supposedly associated with the unusual long spurs of the petals, resembling bird claws or talons.

R-3 CARDINAL FLOWER *(Lobelia cardinalis)* Lobelia family
Height: 2′–3′. Flower: 1½″ long.
Season: Late summer (p.27)

Fortunately this striking flower of the late summer is commonly found in wet situations—along streams and in wet meadows. This has prevented its extinction, since its relative inaccessibility has prevented gross overpicking. The spikelike clusters of brilliant red flowers are found at the ends of unbranched stems with numerous lance-shaped leaves. Hummingbirds are particularly attracted to red flowers, and the tubular blossom is admirably suited for sipping nectar. Its distinct color is responsible for the common name, which likens it to the brilliant red finery of the cardinals of the Roman Church.

4. *Orange Flowers*

O-1   BUTTERFLY WEED *(Asclepias tuberosa)*   Milkweed family
Height: 2′–3′. Flower: ⅜″ diameter; 20–40 in spherical cluster.
Season: Early summer   (p.27)

The spherical cluster of bright-orange flowers is found at the top of a coarse, hairy stem with oblong leaves. The brilliant flowers brighten the dry, open, sandy places that are its natural habitat and are also apparently responsible for the large number of butterflies that visit the plant, hence its common name.

O-2   WOOD LILY *(Lilium philadelphicum)*   Lily family
Height: 1½′–2½′. Flower: 4″ diameter.
Season: Early summer   (p.27)

When seen as a solitary flower in a woodland clearing, we appreciate the beauty of this orange-red lily. The leaves are arranged in whorls along the stem. The petals, mottled with purple-brown spots, are tapered to narrow bases. Thus, even if it rains, the flower head remains erect, since the flower can hold no water.

O-3   TOUCH-ME-NOT *(Impatiens capensis)*   Touch-me-not family
Height: 2′–5′. Flower: 1″ long.
Season: Early summer   (p.28)

These plants are eagerly sought by children, who have learned that touching the mature, bean-shaped seed pod causes them to burst open and scatter their seeds; hence their common and generic (*impatiens*, Latin for "impatient") names. A moist, partially shady habitat is preferred by this plant, where it is seen to grow in fairly large patches. The orange, spurred flowers, mottled with reddish spots, hang on slender branchlets beneath the oval, toothed leaves. The hollow, succulent stem contains a watery juice which soothes the itching of poison ivy.

O-4   HAWKWEED *(Hieracium spp.)*   Composite family
Height: 1′–2′. Flower: ¾″ diameter.
Season: Early summer   (p.28)

This colorful head of flowers on a hairy, leafless stem springs from a basal cluster of hairy, elliptical leaves. The common name refers to the ancient belief that birds of prey ate the plant to strengthen their eyesight. This is also reflected in the generic name, which is derived from the Greek word *hierax*, meaning "hawk." The orange hawkweed, along with the daisy and the yellow hawkweeds, is found in open meadows and fields.

W-1 TRAILING ARBUTUS   p.9

W-2 WOOD ANEMONE   p.11

W-3 RUE ANEMONE   p.9

W-4 DWARF GINSENG   p.10

W-5 BLOODROOT   p.10

W-6 DUTCHMAN'S BREECHES   p.10

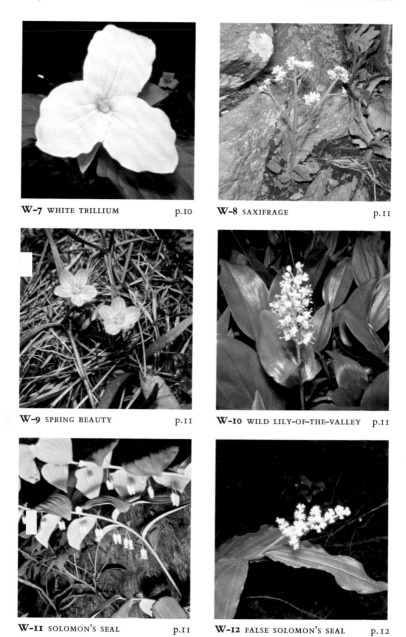

W-7 WHITE TRILLIUM p.10

W-8 SAXIFRAGE p.11

W-9 SPRING BEAUTY p.11

W-10 WILD LILY-OF-THE-VALLEY p.11

W-11 SOLOMON'S SEAL p.11

W-12 FALSE SOLOMON'S SEAL p.12

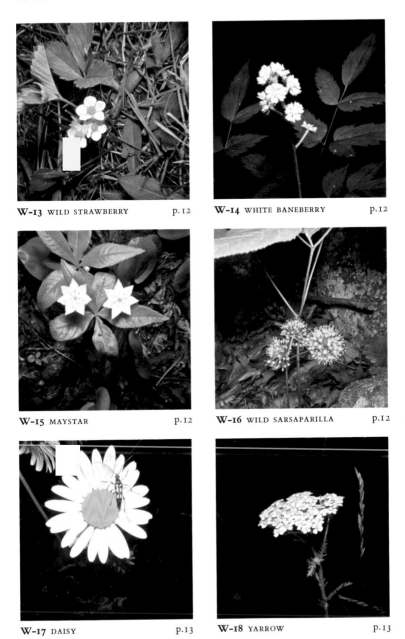

W-13 WILD STRAWBERRY   p. 12

W-14 WHITE BANEBERRY   p. 12

W-15 MAYSTAR   p. 12

W-16 WILD SARSAPARILLA   p. 12

W-17 DAISY   p. 13

W-18 YARROW   p. 13

W-19 FLEABANE   p.13   W-20 MAYAPPLE   p.13

W-21 SPOTTED WINTERGREEN   p.14   W-22 PARTRIDGE BERRY   p.14

W-23 QUEEN ANNE'S LACE   p.14   W-24 HORSE NETTLE   p.14

W-25 TALL MEADOW RUE   p.15

W-26 MEADOWSWEET   p.15

W-27 PEARLY EVERLASTING   p.15

W-28 INDIAN PIPES   p.15

W-29 POKEWEED   p.16

W-30 ARROWHEAD   p.16

W-31 RATTLESNAKE PLANTAIN   p.16   **W-32** BONESET   p.17

W-33 WHITE WOODLAND ASTER   p.17   **W-34** HEATH ASTER   p.17

W-35 TURTLEHEAD   p.17   **G-1** JACK-IN-THE-PULPIT   p.18

G-2 CUCUMBER ROOT   p.18

R-1 RED TRILLIUM   p.19

R-2 WILD COLUMBINE   p.19

R-3 CARDINAL FLOWER   p.19

O-1 BUTTERFLY WEED   p.20

O-2 WOOD LILY   p.20

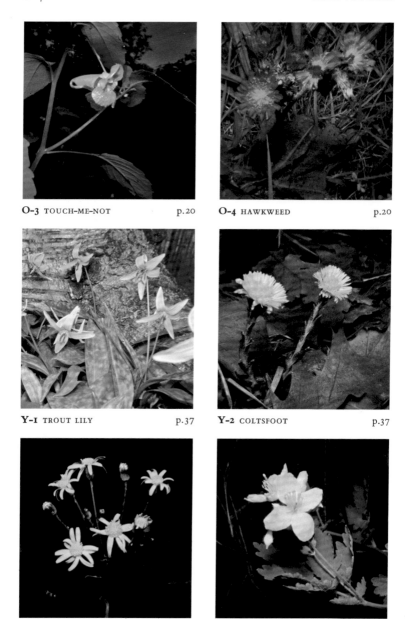

O-3 TOUCH-ME-NOT   p.20

O-4 HAWKWEED   p.20

Y-1 TROUT LILY   p.37

Y-2 COLTSFOOT   p.37

Y-3 GOLDEN RAGWORT   p.37

Y-4 CELADINE   p.38

Y-5 MARSH MARIGOLD   p.38

Y-6 CINQUEFOIL   p.38

Y-7 DANDELION   p.39

Y-8 GOLDSTAR GRASS   p.39

Y-9 BUTTERCUP   p.39

Y-10 BUTTER AND EGGS   p.39

Y-11 BLACK-EYED SUSAN   p.40

Y-12 WHORLED LOOSESTRIFE   p.40

Y-13 ST. JOHNSWORT   p.40

Y-14 COMMON MULLEIN   p.41

Y-15 EVENING PRIMROSE   p.41

Y-16 PARTRIDGE PEA   p.41

Y-17 WILD LETTUCE   p.42

Y-18 GOLDENROD   p.42

Y-19 WILD SUNFLOWER   p.42

B-1 BLUE-EYED GRASS   p.43

B-2 FORGET-ME-NOT   p.43

B-3 DAYFLOWER   p.43

B-4 BLUE VERVAIN   p.44

B-5 CHICORY   p.44

B-6 SQUARE-STEM MONKEY FLOWER   p.44

B-7 FRINGED GENTIAN   p.44

Pi-1 LADY SLIPPER   p.45

Pi-2 STAR THISTLE   p.45

Pi-3 CLOVER   p.45

Pi-4 WILD GERANIUM   p.46

Pi-5 DEPTFORD PINK   p.46

Pi-6 STEEPLEBUSH   p.46

Pi-7 MEADOW BEAUTY   p.46

Pi-8 SMARTWEEDS   p.47

Pi-9 TICK TREFOILS   p.47

Pi-10 MARSH MALLOW   p.47

Pur-1 SKUNK CABBAGE   p.48

Pur-2 LIVERLEAF   p.48

Pur-3 VIOLET   p.48

Pur-4 COW VETCH   p.49

Pur-5 BITTERSWEET NIGHTSHADE p.49

Pur-6 WOOD BETONY p.49

Pur-7 VIRGINIA SPIDERWORT p.49

Pur-8 MILKWEED p.50

Pur-9 PURPLE MILKWORT p.50

Pur-10 HEAL-ALL p.50

Pur-11 PICKERELWEED   p.51

Pur-12 BULL THISTLE   p.51

Pur-13 JOE-PYE-WEED   p.51

Pur-14 IRONWEED   p.52

Pur-15 GREAT LOBELIA   p.52

Pur-16 NEW ENGLAND ASTER   p.52

5. Yellow Flowers

-I   TROUT LILY *(Erythronium americanum)*   Lily family
Height: 6″–9″. Flower: 1″ diameter; nodding.
Season: Early spring   (p.28)

his is a low plant growing in extensive beds in moist woods, often to the exclu-
on of other plants. The leaves are mottled and resemble the marks on a brook
out; hence the common name. Because of these markings and the two upright
nce-shaped leaves, reminding one of alert fawn's ears, this plant is also called
fawn lily." Since several years are necessary for the production of flowers, one
ften finds large flowerless patches of leaves.

Y-2   COLTSFOOT *(Tussilago farfara)*   Composite family
Height: 4″–6″. Flower: 1″ diameter.
Season: Early spring   (p.28)

This flower, found in damp soil along ditches and streams, is often mistaken for
he common dandelion, which it resembles. However, upon close inspection one
inds that the flower stem is scaly and the flowers appear long before the heart-
haped leaves, which are said to resemble the shape of, and to be the size of, a colt's
oot. Hence the common name.

A European immigrant, the plant was brought to this country as a cure for
:oughs (*tussis*, Latin for "cough"). In fact, many generations of New England
:hildren were nursed on coltsfoot-flavored candy sticks when they had a cough
or cold, and the leaves were used as one of the ingredients in herbal tobacco,
which was smoked as a cure for asthma.

Y-3   GOLDEN RAGWORT *(Senecio aureus)*   Composite family
Height: 1′–2′. Flower: ¾″ diameter.
Season: Early spring   (p.28)

Along with the coltsfoot, this is one of the earliest composites to bloom. The
flowers look like small daisies, with nine to twelve yellow petals. Although the
basal leaves of the plant are heart-shaped, the stem leaves are so irregularly toothed
as to give the plant a "ragged" appearance. Look for this plant in moist, open
woods.

Y-4   CELADINE *(Chelidonium majus)*   Poppy famil
Height: 1'–2'. Flower: ½" diameter.
Season: Early spring   (p.28

Another European native that has escaped cultivation, celadine is found in was
places and along roadsides. The compound leaves with numerous lobed an
toothed leaflets are very conspicuous in the early spring, for this is one of th
first plants to emerge. Although the small, four-petal flower does not appear unt
later in the spring, this plant can be easily identified by breaking a piece of th
stem. The broken stem exudes a bright yellow sap that was once used as a prim
itive dye. The common name "celadine" is from the Greek word for "swallow,
because according to the early scholars the mother swallows bathed the eyes c
their young with this sap, thereby strengthening their offspring's eyesight. It wa
also used by herb doctors as a cure for sore eyes.

Y-5   MARSH MARIGOLD *(Caltha palustris)*   Buttercup famil
Height: 8"–18". Flower: 1"–1½" diameter.
Season: Early spring   (p.29

As the common and specific names *(palustris,* Latin for "of swamps") suggest
this plant blooms in marshes and wet woods in early spring. Each flower look
like a large buttercup, and they may grow in such mass profusion that they seem
to pave the marsh with gold. The very conspicuous petals are actually yellow
sepals; this flower has no petals. The stems and heart-shaped leaves were onc
used as a cooked green vegetable, similar to spinach.

Y-6   CINQUEFOIL *(Potentilla spp.)*   Rose family
Height: Species variable. Flower: ½"–¾" diameter.
Season: Early spring   (p.29

The edges of paths or barren fields display the shiny yellow dots of the common
cinquefoil *(P. canadensis* pictured here) even before the grasses are green. There
are many species of this plant, and they vary from a prostrate, creeping vine to a
small shrub; but most are characterized by leaves made of five radiating leaflets;
hence the common name "five fingers," which is derived from the French *cinq
feuilles,* meaning "five leaves." Its habit of developing creeping runners often
leads one to confuse this plant with the wild strawberry. However, the wild
strawberry has white flowers and leaves made of three leaflets.

Y-7   DANDELION *(Taraxacum officinale)*   Composite family
Height: 2″–6″. Flower: 1″–1½″ diameter.
Season: Early spring   (p.29)

This ubiquitous plant springs from a large, tough root and is therefore very difficult to remove from a lawn or field, which is its preferred habitat. Although it is a scourge to the suburbanite trying to maintain a beautiful lawn, its leaves are much prized by some people as a salad green. The leaves are also responsible for its common name, which is a corruption of the French *dent de lion*, in reference to the leaf's jagged edge, resembling the teeth of a lion. The feathery, tufted seeds form downy balls, which are a delight to children and a vexation to the golfer trying to find his ball on a dandelion-infested fairway.

Y-8   GOLDSTAR GRASS *(Hypoxis hirsuta)*   Amaryllis family
Height: 4″–6″. Flower: ¾″ diameter.
Season: Spring   (p.29)

The generic name of this plant tells us that its preferred habitat is acid soil *(hypoxys,* Latin for "somewhat acid") in grasslands or open woods. The leaves are grasslike and are longer than the flowering stem. Each blossom is composed of three petals and three sepals, but since they are the same color and size, the flower is a six-pointed yellow star.

Y-9   BUTTERCUP *(Ranunculus spp.)*   Buttercup family
Height: Species variable. Flower: ¾″–1″ diameter.
Season: Spring   (p.29)

As its generic name suggests *(ranunculus,* Latin for "little frog"), the buttercup is usually found in a moist habitat. Although there are thirty-seven species of this plant in the United States, the buttercup is easily recognized even by children. The butter-yellow reflection of the shiny, waxy petals when the flower is held under the chin always gives an affirmative answer to the query, "Do you like butter?" However, cows are poisoned if they eat the plant.

Y-10   BUTTER AND EGGS *(Linaria vulgaris)*   Figwort family
Height: 8″–16″. Flower: 1″ long.
Season: Early summer   (p.29)

A common inhabitant of waste places and roadsides, this plant was brought from Europe because it yielded a skin lotion used by the early settlers. The flowers, clustered at the top of a single stem with many narrow, bluish-green leaves, resemble the blossoms of the cultivated snapdragon. Like the snapdragon, the flower has two lips and a long spur. The "butter"-yellow flower has an orange blotch ("eggs") on its lower lip.

Y-11 BLACK-EYED SUSAN *(Rudbeckia serotina)* Composite family
Height: 1'–3'. Flower: 3" diameter.
Season: Early summer (p.30)

Along with the daisy, this plant is a common inhabitant of the open meadows. Originally a native of the western United States, the plant was introduced into this part of the country in samples of clover seed. It is a rough plant with hairy stems and hairy, club-shaped leaves. Being a member of the composite family, it has yellow ray flowers and purplish-brown disk flowers. The disk becomes cone-shaped as it matures; hence another common name for these plants is "cone-flower."

Y-12 WHORLED LOOSESTRIFE *(Lysimachia quadrifolia)*
Height: 1'–3'. Flower: ⅝" diameter. Primrose family
Season: Early summer (p.30)

The generic name of these plants honors Lysimachus, King of Sicily, who, according to tradition, used the plant to pacify an angry bull that was chasing him, i.e., he released the bull from his strife! This tradition held until fairly recent times, when the plant was fed to teams of oxen in the belief that it pacified the animals and caused them to work harmoniously together. The plant is characterized by whorls of yellow flowers streaked with red, arising from whorls of lance-shaped leaves at regular intervals along the stem.

Y-13 ST. JOHNSWORT *(Hypericum spp.)* St. Johnswort family
Height: 1'–3'. Flower: ¾" diameter.
Season: Early summer (p.30)

These immigrants brought with them all of the mystery and superstition that surrounded them in Europe. The plants, which were gathered on St. John's eve, June 24, were hung in the doors and windows of homes to ward off evil spirits and protect from lightning. Ointments and potions made from the plant and applied to wounds presumably led to quick healing. It was considered a potent stimulant and was used in treating depression. The more than twenty-five species found in this country soon became established in open waste fields. The fuzzy appearance of the flower is due to the numerous stamens which occupy its center. Also notice that the stemless leaves, and sometimes even the petals, have small black dots which are actually small chambers containing oil. Hold a leaf up to the sunlight and notice that these dots appear translucent.

Y-14 COMMON MULLEIN *(Verbascum thapus)* Figwort family
Height: 2′–7′. Flower: ½″ diameter.
Season: Early summer (p.30)

This biennial grows a basal rosette of large woolly leaves its first year; during the second year it produces a tall stalk with many large woolly leaves topped by a cylindrical spike containing buds, flowers, and seeds. The plant is rather unattractive, since only a few flowers appear at one time, so that the flower spike, which continues to grow all summer, carries dead flowers in addition to full and empty dry seed pods. However, this plant was much used by man. The ancient Romans dipped the dried stalks in suet and used them as torches in funeral processions, and the Greeks used the leaves as lamp wicks. The leaves, steeped as tea or mixed with tobacco to be smoked, were used as a cure for lung diseases. Indians used the leaves as inner soles in moccasins; the early settlers lined their stockings with the leaves to keep their feet warm; and even Quaker maidens, who were forbidden to use any type of makeup, used to rub their cheeks with the leaves, the slight abrasive quality causing an attractive reddening. Hail the "flannel leaf"!

Y-15 EVENING PRIMROSE *(Oenotheria biennis)*
Height: 2′–5′. Flower: 1″–1½″ diameter. Evening-primrose family
Season: Summer (p.30)

A biennial found in dry ground in open meadows and along roadways, the evening primrose is a tall weed with narrow, pointed leaves growing alternately along the stem. The four-petal flowers found at the end of the stem usually open near sunset for one night only, new ones opening each evening. They fill the night air with the fragrance of lemons.

Y-16 PARTRIDGE PEA *(Cassia fasciculata)* Bean family
Height: 6″–18″. Flower: 1″–1½″ diameter.
Season: Summer (p.30)

This is one of the so-called "sensitive" plants. The leaves of these plants, which consist of ten to fifteen pairs of small leaflets, fold up at night and open again in the morning sun. The plant prefers a dry, sandy soil, which is manifested by the fact that it is one of the first plants to grow in an area in which the topsoil has been removed for a gravel pit. Being a member of the bean family, it produces a rather conspicuous seed pod containing seeds which are relished by gamebirds.

Y-17   WILD LETTUCE *(Lactuca spp.)*   Composite family
            Height: 3′–10′. Flower: ⅜″ diameter.
            Season: Late summer   (p.31)

Although the flowers of this plant are quite small and inconspicuous, the great
height of many of these plants form a conspicuous part of wet and open thickets
during the late summer. If at a distance you see a tall plant with large, deeply
lobed, lance-shaped leaves topped with a large number of conspicuous fuzzy
balls, actually a collection of feathery, tufted seeds, you have found a wild lettuce.
On close inspection you will find small yellow or blue flowers. If you remove a
leaf, you will notice that the stem "bleeds" a milky juice, which accounts for its
generic name *(lac*, Latin for "milk").

Y-18   GOLDENROD *(Solidago spp.)*   Composite family
            Height: 2′–4′. Flower: ⅛″-¼″ long; variously shaped clusters.
            Season: Late summer   (p.31)

In the late summer and early fall the meadows and roadsides glow with the
radiant yellows of the tiny flowers that make up the flower heads of goldenrod.
Everyone recognizes goldenrod, with its alternate leaves, but species identification is difficult, since there are at least 75 species of this plant, more than 40 species
being found in the northeast. This plant has gained some notoriety through the
years. Its beauty has earned it a place as the state flower of Alabama, Kentucky,
and Nebraska. Its reputed healing powers are responsible for its generic designa-
tion, since *solidus* is Latin for "whole," in other words, "to make whole." It has
been vilified as a causative agent in hay fever, although recent evidence indicates
that the pollen of goldenrod is too heavy to be windborne; it is actually the
inconspicuous flowers of the ragweed, which blooms at the same time as goldenrod, that are the principal culprit during the fall "sneeze season."

Y-19   WILD SUNFLOWER *(Helianthus spp.)*   Composite family
            Height: 3′–12′. Flower: 2½″–3″ diameter.
            Season: Late summer   (p.31)

There are approximately one hundred species of sunflower. The generic name is
a combination of two Greek words—*helios* ("sun") and *anthos* ("flower"). The
early Incas worshiped this flower as a symbol of the sun. The plant is found in wet
meadows and moist ground, where the yellow-rayed flowers are displayed con-
spicuously on tall stems. The leaves of most sunflowers are characterized by two
prominent veins coming from the midrib near its base. Wild sunflower seeds
provide valuable nutrients for various kinds of animal life.

Other flowers, certain species or varieties of which may appear yellow:
violet, hawkweeds, clover, and wood betony.

6. Blue Flowers

B-1   BLUE-EYED GRASS *(Sisyrinchium spp.)*   Iris family
Height: 6″–12″. Flower: ½″–¾″ diameter.
Season: Early summer   (p.31)

This delicate flower is a rather subdued member of the flamboyant iris family. It is found in moist meadows and open fields, where its dark-green, grasslike leaves blend in with the other grasses present. The starlike flower is composed of three petals and three petal-like sepals, all of which end in a pointed tip. These flowers last only one day and open only in bright sunlight.

B-2   FORGET-ME-NOT *(Myosotis scorpioides)*   Borage family
Height: Sprawling 12″–18″. Flower: ⅓″ diameter.
Season: Early summer   (p.31)

A symbol of love, this perennial of European origin is found along the swampy margins of streams and in wet meadows. The common name comes from an incident in German folk history, in which a knight who was drowning in a stream tossed a sprig of this plant to his distraught lover, who was helplessly standing on the bank, crying, "Forget me not." Although the plant can grow to one and one-half feet in length, it is usually seen as a sprawling, tangled mass of lance-shaped leaves. The specific name, *scorpioides* (Latin for "scorpionlike"), refers to the flower stems, which are curved around like the tail of a scorpion.

B-3   DAYFLOWER *(Commelina communis)*   Spiderwort family
Height: Sprawling 1′–2′. Flower: ½″ diameter.
Season: Early summer   (p.31)

Like its close relative the spiderwort, the dayflower blooms only a few hours before dying, and then only on warm, sunny days. A native of Asia, this plant escaped cultivation and now grows successfully in cool woods or along the banks of streams. The bases of its lance-shaped leaves clasp the jointed stem of this sprawling perennial. The flower, with its two prominent blue petals and one small, inconspicuous, faded petal, is responsible for the generic name of this plant. Linnaeus, the famous plant taxonomist, dedicated the plant to the three Commelin brothers: two were notable botanists, and the third "died before accomplishing anything in botany."

B-4   BLUE VERVAIN *(Verbena hastata)*   Verbena family
Height: 4'–6'. Flower: ¼" diameter; few on a slender spike.
Season: Summer   (p.32)

These plants, with pairs of toothed, lance-shaped leaves along their tall stems, are found along ponds and lakes and in damp, open woods. The thin flower spikes are never in full bloom; only a small ring of tiny blossoms is open at any one time. The generic name *Verbena* is the Latin name for any sacred herb. Because of this reputation, it was much sought after by herb doctors.

B-5   CHICORY *(Cichorium intybus)*   Composite family
Height: 1'–3'. Flower: 1½"–2".
Season: Summer   (p.32)

This handsome flower but noxious weed is found along roadsides and in waste places. The basal rosette of leaves eventually gives rise to rank stems with small, lance-shaped leaves. The flowers open at sunrise and close by noon and seldom open at all if the day is cloudy. The plant was brought to this country from Europe, where its dried and ground root was used to improve the flavor of coffee.

B-6   SQUARE-STEM MONKEY FLOWER *(Mimulus ringens)*
Height: 1'–3'. Flower: ½"–¾" diameter.   Figwort family
Season: Summer   (p.32)

Taxonomists saw a resemblance between this grinning, flop-eared flower and the head of a monkey, the natural buffoon *(mimus,* Latin for "buffoon"). The square stems (feel them!) have pairs of opposite, coarsely toothed, lance-shaped leaves. The flowers arise from the stem, where the upper leaves meet the stem. Look for this plant along the banks of streams and in swamps and wet fields.

B-7   FRINGED GENTIAN *(Gentiana crinita)*   Gentian family
Height: 6"–12". Flower: 1"–2" length.
Season: Fall   (p.32)

When almost all the other flowers have died and gone to seed, the beautiful gentian begins to bloom and continues to produce flowers until the first heavy frost. The stems, with opposite, oval leaves, are topped with dark-blue flowers composed of four fringed petals. Its natural habitat is cool, damp thickets and meadows. The roots of some species of this plant once had medicinal value. This was discovered by Gentius, King of Illyria, an ancient country along the Adriatic Sea, hence the common and generic name.

Other flowers, certain species or varieties of which may appear blue: wild lettuce, liverleaf, cow vetch, great lobelia, and fleabane.

7. Pink Flowers

Pi-1 LADY SLIPPER *(Cypripedium acuale)* Orchid family
Height: 8″–12″. Flower: 2″ long.
Season: Spring (p.32)

The bleakness of the woods and bogs in which this plant grows accentuates its elegant beauty. The showy pink flower emerges between two hairy, basal leaves. The "slipper" is a saclike petal with a longitudinal cleft. If an insect lands on this cleft it drops into the sac, and the only way out is through the two openings at the rear of the "slipper." But in passing through these openings the insect brushes against the reproductive organs located here, thus ensuring pollination. Look for this flower off the beaten path, since ruthless picking has made it a rarity in areas traversed by many people.

Pi-2 STAR THISTLE *(Centaurea cyanus)* Composite family
Height: 2′–4′. Flower: 1½″–2″ diameter.
Season: Spring (p.32)

This thornless thistle is a European import that has escaped cultivation. It is a bushy-appearing plant with small, oblong leaves and is usually found along roadsides and in open meadows, where it blooms continuously until late summer. Another common name for this plant is "bachelor's button," which refers to the charming practice of a bygone era when English maidens wore the flower as a sign that they were eligible for marriage.

Pi-3 CLOVER *(Trifolium spp.)* Bean family
Height: 8″–15″. Flower: ⅜″ long; many in a globular head.
Season: Spring (p.33)

The common clover is a rather uncommon plant. The generic name refers to the characteristic three oblong leaflets that go to make up the leaf, which some people claim is the true shamrock of Ireland. The plant, which produces flowers of various colors, not only adds beauty to the lawns and meadows in which it grows; its root system harbors nitrogen-fixing bacteria, which add nutrients to the soil. The word "clover" is derived from the Latin *clava*, meaning "clubs." This is in reference to the three-knobbed club of Hercules, which the leaves were thought to resemble. The next time you play cards, take a close look at the symbol for clubs.

Pi-4   WILD GERANIUM *(Geranium maculatum)*   Geranium family
Height: 1'–2'. Flower: 1"–1½" diameter.
Season: Spring   (p.33)

A patch of wild geranium adds a bright spot to an otherwise bleak, sparsely leafed, spring woodland. The soft-pink flowers and broad, finely cut leaves give the plant a delicate appearance in the coarse surroundings. The shape of the seed pod is responsible for the common and generic names of this plant, since it is said to resemble the beak of a crane (*geranos*, Greek for "crane").

Pi-5   DEPTFORD PINK *(Dianthus armeria)*   Pink family
Height: 8"–24". Flower: ½" diameter.
Season: Early summer   (p.33)

What could Jupiter (*Dianthus*, Greek for "Jupiter's flower") have seen in this grasslike plant with small leaves and fairly inconspicuous flowers growing along roadsides and dry places? Close inspection reveals a delicate pink flower mottled with white dots and having "pinked" petals—a wise choice by the chief of the Roman gods. The common name refers to its European origin, since it once grew in abundance in Deptford, England.

Pi-6   STEEPLEBUSH *(Spiraea tomentosa)*   Rose family
Height: 2'–4'. Flower: ¼" diameter; spikelike cluster.
Season: Summer   (p.33)

Steeplebush is found in moist meadows and wooded fields along with its close relative the meadowsweet. It can be distinguished from meadowsweet by the spirelike arrangement of its pink blossoms and its ovate leaves with very hairy undersurfaces. The undersurfaces of these leaves are so woolly that they are responsible for the specific name *tomentose*, Latin for "cushion stuffing."

Pi-7   MEADOW BEAUTY *(Rhexia virginica)*   Melastoma family
Height: 1'–2'. Flower: 1" diameter.
Season: Summer   (p.33)

The meadow beauty is a fugitive from the tropics. The Melastoma family is almost entirely tropical, with the exception of *Rhexia*. The flower is unique because of its unusually long and curved yellow anthers. The plant grows in moist, sandy, open woods or meadows, where the brilliant pink flowers sparkle from the tops of square stems with stemless, opposite, oval leaves. Because it is relished as food by deer, it is also called "deergrass."

Pi-8   SMARTWEEDS *(Polygonum spp.)*   Buckwheat family
Height: Variable. Flower: ⅛″–³⁄₁₆″ diameter; many in spikelike cluster.
Season: Summer   (p.33)

There are a great many species of this ubiquitous plant. Many species are found near or in water. Most species have pink flowers, but some may bear white blossoms. One group has curved prickles on its stems and is called "tearthumbs." Another common name, "knotweeds," is derived from the generic name (*poly*, Latin for "many"; *gonu*, Latin for "joint" or "knee"), which refers to the many swollen joints that are characteristic of the stems of these plants. Another characteristic is the presence of a sheath at the junction of the leaf with the stem. The spikelike cluster of flowers eventually gives rise to seeds relished as food by gamebirds.

Pi-9   TICK TREFOILS *(Desmodium spp.)*   Bean family
Height: 2′–5′. Flower: ½″–¾″ length.
Season: Summer   (p.34)

We might not pay any attention to this rank weed except that during the late summer and the fall a walk through the open woods usually ends with time being spent removing the small, roughly triangular seed pods from clothing. The seed pods, which are connected in groups containing two to five units (*desmos*, Greek for "chain"), have hooked bristles which easily catch and cling to clothing and animal hair. There are many species of this plant which in addition to having the unique seed pods are also characterized by small pealike flowers and compound leaves composed of three leaflets (trefoil).

Pi-10   MARSH MALLOW *(Hibiscus palustris)*   Mallow family
Height: 4′–6′. Flower: 6″ diameter.
Season: Late summer   (p.34)

The mallows can be easily recognized by the peculiar structure in the center of the flower—many stamens projecting from a central stalk like the bristles in a bottle brush. The marsh, or rose, mallow has tall canelike stems with pointed, ovate leaves. The delicate though large flowers of this plant seem out of place in the hostile environment of a swamp or marsh. The root of one of the European members of this family was the original source of the material that was used to make the favorite campfire confection—marshmallows.

Other flowers, certain species or varieties of which may appear pink: spring beauty, white trillium, fleabanes, trailing arbutus, turtlehead, cow vetch, and milkwort.

8. *Purple Flowers*

Pur-1   SKUNK CABBAGE *(Symplocarpus foetidus)*   Arum family
            Height: 4″–6″. Flower: tiny, in a knoblike spike surrounded by a spathe.
            Season: Early spring   (p.34)

The traditional heralds of spring, these are the first flowers to emerge; in fact, they may have started the previous fall. It is not unusual to walk in the woods following a snowstorm in February or March and see the flower of skunk cabbage poking through the snow. These plants are found in depressions and hollows in the open woods wherever there is an abundance of soil water. The small inconspicuous flowers are arranged on a knoblike spike enclosed within a yellow-dappled, dark-purple, hoodlike spathe. Breaking the spathe or leaves gives the characteristic skunk odor (*foetidus*, Latin for "foul-smelling").

Pur-2   LIVERLEAF *(Hepatica americana)*   Buttercup family
            Height: 4″–6″. Flower: ½″ diameter.
            Season: Early spring   (p.34)

Another, almost incongruous herald of spring is the delicate flower of the liverleaf. Toward the end of March, the fragile-looking flowers with their conspicuous petal-like sepals push their way up through the debris that covers the wooded slopes on which they are found. The new leaves appear later in the spring. The shape of the leaf is the reason for the common and generic names of this plant. It was thought to resemble the three-lobed mammalian liver (*hepaticus*, Latin for "pertaining to the liver"). Herb doctors who practiced their art according to the "doctrine of signatures" used this plant to treat liver ailments.

Pur-3   VIOLET *(Viola spp.)*   Violet family
            Height: 4″–6″. Flower: ¾″–1¼″ diameter.
            Season: Early spring   (p.34)

Another flower closely associated with the early spring is the violet. There are many species of violet, and most are found in rich open woods or the edge of meadows. Although the purple meadow violets are conspicuous by their size and numbers, the earliest violet to bloom in Connecticut is a small yellow violet of the woodlands. Many violets produce showy sterile flowers, the fertile ones being closed, self-pollinating, inconspicuous, budlike flowers found at the base of the plant. Cut-up violet flowers are used by some people as a decorative garnish on salads, where they not only provide color but also are a concentrated source of vitamin C.

Pur-4 COW VETCH *(Vicia cracca)* Bean family
Height: Climbing. Flower: ½″ long.
Season: Spring (p.34)

A common inhabitant of waste places and fields, this plant was brought to this country from Europe as a forage crop for cattle. It grows in patches, the dark-green leaves composed of eight to twelve pairs of leaflets and the hanging clusters of purple flowers calling it to our attention. It has often been plowed under as a "green manure," since its roots contain nitrogen-fixing bacteria which produce nitrates, a valuable plant nutrient.

Pur-5 BITTERSWEET NIGHTSHADE *(Solanum dulcamara)*
Height: Climbing vine. Flower: ½″ diameter. Nightshade family
Season: Spring (p.35)

Another European import that has invaded thickets and fence rows is the bitter-sweet nightshade. The vine is rather handsome—ovate, alternate leaves with two conspicuous lobes at their bases, and a cone of yellow stamens in the center of the purple star-shaped flower. However, the leaves of this plant are poisonous, as is the fruit. The common name is attributable to a report by early botanists that the chewed root first tasted bitter, then sweet.

Pur-6 WOOD BETONY *(Pedicularis canadensis)* Figwort family
Height: 6″–10″. Flower: ¾″ long.
Season: Spring (p.35)

Even though it doesn't bloom until May, this plant is often conspicuous in April because of its rosette of very unusual fernlike leaves. The purple or yellow flowers are found in clusters at the top of a common stalk. A popular name for this plant is "lousewort," from the European belief that cattle that grazed near them became infested with lice. The generic name also reflects this belief *(pedicularis,* Latin for "louse"). Look for these plants in open woods and clearings.

Pur-7 VIRGINIA SPIDERWORT *(Tradescantia virginiana)*
Height: 1′–2′. Flower: 1″–1½″ diameter. Spiderwort family
Season: Spring (p.35)

Morning is the only time to look for this flower, since it usually closes by noon. The flowers are interspersed throughout the masses of long, tapering, grasslike leaves, whose angular growth suggests spider legs. The center of the three-petal flower also contains long filaments covered with fuzzy hair, again suggesting a spider; hence the common name. The plant prefers partial shade and is found in thickets and open woods and meadows. The generic name honors John Trades-cant, a botanist and gardener to Charles I of England.

Pur-8 MILKWEED *(Asclepias spp.)*   Milkweed family
Height: 3′–5′. Flower: ½″ diameter; spherical cluster.
Season: Early summer   (p.35)

There are about twenty-five species of milkweeds in the eastern United States, most of which bear flowers that are some shade of purple or red. In general the plants are characterized by leaves that are usually oval or lance-shaped, arranged in pairs along a stem that bleeds a milky sap when broken. Habitat varies with species from dry, open places to swamps, where you find the swamp milkweed (*A. incarnata*), illustrated here. During the fall the seed pod of the plants commands our attention because of its seeds with long, silky hairs. Early settlers in this country used this hair to stuff pillows and mattresses, and during World War I children were paid a penny a pound for milkweed "silk," to be used to stuff life preservers when the regular material used was no longer available.

Pur-9 PURPLE MILKWORT *(Polygala sanguinea)*   Milkwort family
Height: 6″–12″. Flower: ¼″ long; oval cluster.
Season: Early summer   (p.35)

This small annual is found in moist meadows in acid soil, where its flower is often mistaken for clover. However, close inspection will reveal not the typical clover-leaf but small, narrow leaves. The common name refers not to a milky sap but to the ancient belief that dairy cattle fed this plant increased their flow of milk. This belief is reflected in the Greek derivation of its generic name *polys*, meaning "much"; and *gala*, meaning "milk." The plant is also called "candyroot" because the crushed root has a wintergreen flavor.

Pur-10 HEAL-ALL *(Prunella vulgaris)*   Mint family
Height: 4″–8″. Flower: ½″ long; many on a blunt spike.
Season: Summer   (p.35)

Another European plant brought to this country by the early herb doctors was the heal-all. It had an outstanding reputation in Europe as a medicinal herb. It was applied to all types of wounds in England, and the French had a proverb which said that if one had heal-all one had no need for a surgeon. The generic name is a corruption of the German word *Brunelle*, which means "quinsy," a type of fever that was supposed to be cured by the herb. Being a member of the mint family, the plant has the typical square stem with opposite, oval leaves. It can be found along roadsides and in fields.

Pur-11 PICKERELWEED *(Pontederia cordata)*   Pickerelweed family
Height: 1′–2′. Flower: ⅜″ long; many on a spike.
Season: Summer   (p.36)

This plant grows in the shallow, quiet waters of lakes, streams, and ponds favored by pickerel; hence its common name. The flower stalk and single heart-shaped leaf *(chorda*, Latin for "heart") sometimes form an almost impenetrable barrier above the surface of the water, which is a bane to boatmen and fishermen who try to use these waters. However, the flowers produce seeds in the fall that serve as food for wild ducks.

Pur-12 BULL THISTLE *(Cirsium vulgare)*   Composite family
Height: 3′–5′. Flower: 2″–3″ diameter.
Season: Summer   (p.36)

When one looks at a thistle, one thinks, "Pins and needles." The stems, lobed leaves, and even the flowers of this biennial plant contain sharp prickles. The common bull thistle is of European origin and quickly spread in this country, where it is found in meadows, waste places, and along roadsides. The plumed seeds, which appear in late summer and fall, are relished as food by the goldfinch.

This plant was used by herb doctors, who believed in the "doctrine of signatures." If you look at the underside of the leaves of these plants you will notice that the vein in the midline is bulged along its entire length. Some herb doctors saw this as a varicose vein and used the plant for treating this condition. This practice is reflected in its generic name *cirsos*, Greek for "swollen vein."

Pur-13 JOE-PYE-WEED *(Eupatorium maculatum)*   Composite family
Height: 3′–5′. Flower: ½″ long; many in a flat head.
Season: Late summer   (p.36)

The heralds of fall are the yellow of the goldenrod and the purple wine-stain color of the Joe-Pye-weed. This tall plant with whorled, coarsely toothed, oval leaves grows in wet meadows and roadside ditches. The flowers are so similar to those of boneset in both size and shape that this plant is often called "purple boneset." The reputed healing powers of this plant are also legend. The generic name honors the herb doctor Eupator, who used this plant during biblical times. During colonial times in New England an Indian herb doctor called Joe Pye was said to have used this plant to stem a typhus-fever epidemic in Massachusetts.

Pur-14 IRONWEED *(Veronia noveboracensis)*   Composite family
      Height: 4'–6'. Flower: 1"–1½" diameter; several in open, flat cluster.
      Season: Late summer   (p.36)

This plant appears at the same time and same places as the Joe-Pye-weed, but they can never be confused because of the difference in coloration of the flowers. Ironweed is a deep purple, in contrast to the dull wine-stain color of Joe-Pye-weed. This is not evident in color pictures, because ironweed photographs a dark pink no matter what type of film is used. Look for this tall plant with alternate, narrow, finely toothed leaves in damp thickets and meadows.

Pur-15 GREAT LOBELIA *(Lobelia syphilitica)*   Lobelia family
      Height: 1'–3'. Flower: 1" long; many in a spike.
      Season: Late summer   (p.36)

This lobelia, in contrast to its much more flamboyant relative, the cardinal flower, is not seen as readily because of its subdued color and its habit of growing with other plants that may be as tall as or taller than it. This secretive plant, with its alternate, lance-shaped leaves tapering at both ends, grows in wet meadows and along the banks of streams. The specific name is due to the belief that the roots of this plant could be used as a treatment for syphilis.

Pur-16 NEW ENGLAND ASTER *(Aster novae-angliae)* Composite family
      Height: 4'–8'. Flower: 1½"–2" diameter.
      Season: Late summer   (p.36)

There are many species of aster which produce flowers with various hues of purple. The most conspicuous and certainly the most beautiful one found in Connecticut is the New England aster. It is usually found in wet meadows or swampy places. The tall stems, with stalkless, lance-shaped leaves, are topped by flowers composed of deep-purple ray flowers and brilliant orange-yellow disk flowers. It is surprising that this magnificent wild flower was not adopted by any of the New England states as its state flower.

Other flowers, certain species or varieties of which may appear purple: star thistle, clover, blue vervain, blue-eyed grass, and smartweed.

Appendix

EARLY SPRING March–early May

White
Trailing Arbutus
Rue Anemone
Wood Anemone
Dwarf Ginseng
Bloodroot
Dutchman's Breeches
Saxifrage
Spring Beauty

Yellow
Trout Lily
Coltsfoot
Golden Ragwort
Marsh Marigold
Cinquefoil
Dandelion

Purple
Skunk Cabbage
Violet
Liverleaf

SPRING May–mid-June

White
Wild Lily-of-the-valley
Solomon's Seal
False Solomon's Seal
Wild Strawberry
Maystar
Wild Sarsaparilla
Daisy
Yarrow
Fleabane
Mayapple
White Trillium
White Baneberry

Green
Jack-in-the-pulpit
Cucumber Root

Red
Wild Columbine
Red Trillium

Yellow
Butter and Eggs
Celadine
Goldstar Grass
Buttercup

Pink
Lady Slipper
Star Thistle
Clover
Wild Geranium

Purple
Cow Vetch
Bittersweet Nightshade
Wood Betony
Virginia Spiderwort

EARLY SUMMER mid-June–mid-July

White
Spotted Wintergreen
Partridge Berry
Queen Anne's Lace
Horse Nettle

Orange
Touch-me-not
Hawkweed

Yellow
Black-eyed Susan
Whorled Loosestrife
St. Johnswort
Common Mullein

Blue
Blue-eyed Grass
Forget-me-not
Dayflower

Pink
Deptford Pink

Purple
Milkweed
Purple Milkwort
Heal-all

SUMMER mid-July–August

White
Meadowsweet
Boneset
Pearly Everlasting
Indian Pipes
Arrowhead
Rattlesnake Plantain
Tall Meadow Rue
Pokeweed

Orange
Butterfly Weed
Wood Lily

Yellow
Evening Primrose
Partridge Pea

Blue
Blue Vervain
Square-stem
   Monkey Flower
Chicory

Pink
Meadow Beauty
Steeplebush
Smartweeds
Tick Trefoils

Purple
Pickerelweed
Bull Thistle

LATE SUMMER August–September

White
White Woodland Aster
Heath Aster
Turtlehead

Red
Cardinal Flower

Yellow
Wild Sunflower
Goldenrod
Wild Lettuce

Pink
Marsh Mallow

Purple
Joe-Pye-weed
Ironweed
Great Lobelia
New England Aster

FALL mid-September–October

Blue
Fringed Gentian

Index of Common Names

The first page reference is for text; the second is for illustration.

Index of Scientific Names

The first page reference is for text; the second is for illustration.